Original title:
Under the Canopy of Home

Copyright © 2025 Creative Arts Management OÜ
All rights reserved.

Author: Aidan Marlowe
ISBN HARDBACK: 978-1-80581-772-7
ISBN PAPERBACK: 978-1-80581-299-9
ISBN EBOOK: 978-1-80581-772-7

Shaded Haven of Joy and Rest

In a nook where the squirrels play,
Sunbeams dance at the end of day.
A chair so comfy, a drink in hand,
I'll stay forever, this is my land.

The grass tickles my toes, oh so fine,
An old dog snores, dreaming of wine.
Birds sing a tune, a sweet silly song,
In this snug corner, we all belong.

Canvas of Shadows and Sunbeams

The umbrella's up, but I'm stuck in the chair,
With lemonade spills and a bee in my hair.
A picnic blanket, crumbs everywhere,
Telling old jokes with no worries or care.

Sunlight creeps in with a cheeky grin,
While ants declare a humorous win.
They march in a line, so proud and so neat,
I toss them a crumb, they dance on my feet.

The Heartfelt Whisper of Nature

The whispering leaves share secrets they know,
About the neighbor's cat, and the time it got slow.
A breeze tickles my neck, a soft little tease,
While clouds overhead get plush like a sneeze.

A butterfly lands on my nose for a chat,
I laugh till I snort at the sight of that brat.
The world is a circus, nature's own jest,
With laughter and joy, this moment's the best.

Journeying Through Leafy Labyrinths

Wandering paths made of twigs and of leaves,
I dodge a downpour, oh how nature weaves.
A map in my hand, but it's upside down,
I take the wrong turn and end up in town.

With each twist and turn, a new friend appears,
A wise old turtle courts doubts and fears.
In this maze of fun, I giggle and roam,
For lost in the wild, I've still found my home.

Nestled in the Nature of Us

In a treehouse brave and tall,
We argue who will take the fall.
While squirrels watch with cheeky grins,
We plot and scheme, let chaos begin.

With branches strong, we swing and sway,
Our laughter brightens every day.
The acorn fights, it can't compete,
Our giggles make the world so sweet.

Blossoms of Togetherness

In gardens lush, we plant our seeds,
But weeds come back with greater deeds.
The daisies think they own the space,
While we just laugh, it's all a race.

The tulips snicker, dressed so grand,
As petals fall from our shaky hands.
We dance in mud, slip and slide,
What blooms next is our silly pride.

Whispers of Time Passed

As fireflies flicker in the night,
We misplace shoes, oh what a sight!
The stars above wink with delight,
While we search for our snacks, what a plight!

Old stories told with much exaggeration,
Our youth spent in strange collaboration.
A treasure map to lost old socks,
We dig up memories like buried rocks.

Beauty Beneath the Bow

Beneath the branches, we play hide and seek,
Falling over roots, tripping on squeaks.
With cartoon birds, our minds dance free,
Imagining a world where all is silly glee.

We giggle like children, unbothered by time,
With silly hopscotch drawn in chalk lines.
A picnic spread where ants have feasts,
In the wild laughter, our joy never ceased.

Refuge Among the Bowing Branches

Squirrels argue over acorns,
While birds play tag in the breeze.
A raccoon peeks from a shadow,
Claiming snacks with such ease.

Laughter echoes through the leaves,
As frogs croak their silly tunes.
A fox in shades of orange prances,
Beneath the watchful moon.

Heartbeats in Nature's Cloak

Bees buzz like they're gossiping,
While rabbits dance to the sound.
A turtle tries to keep up pace,
Whispers in the grass abound.

Sunshine tickles every blade,
And shadows play a game of peek.
The owl rolls his big ol' eyes,
At all the mischiefs of the week.

The Embrace of Time-worn Boughs

Old trees are ancient comedians,
With branches waving at the sky.
They tell tales of stormy nights,
And laughter from passersby.

Mice play hide and seek with nuts,
While crickets chirp in delight.
In this whimsical, wild warm-up,
The day turns into night.

Hideaway in the Green Embrace

Frogs leap like they're in a race,
While lizards bask, oh so cool.
There's a picnic of ants feasting,
Next to a small, playful pool.

The wind whispers silly secrets,
To the flowers, soft and sweet.
In this realm of carefree antics,
Nature's laughs never miss a beat.

Candles of Belonging

In the kitchen, smoke alarms sing,
Chasing the cat while I burn the spring.
Pancakes flip like a circus act,
Maple syrup is my sticky pact.

Mom's laughter echoes through the halls,
As we dodge the bouncing tennis balls.
Family games, oh what a sight,
Who knew scrabble would end in a fight?

Socks all mismatched, a family trend,
Like crazy puzzle pieces, we blend.
The dog steals snacks, he's in high demand,
In this funny home, we all take a stand.

With candles lit and jokes at play,
Each shared moment brightens the day.
Amidst the chaos, love does thrive,
In this madcap home, we come alive.

The Framework of Love's Canopy

Building walls made of laughter sounds,
The roof's a quilt with silly bounds.
Nail on a smile, paint it bright,
In this odd house, we find delight.

Grandpa's stories go on for hours,
He swears that gum gives you super powers.
We gather 'round, popcorn in hand,
As he spins tales that go unplanned.

Chairs all wobble, a strange parade,
One wrong move, and a seat gets made.
With each clatter, we burst into glee,
In this quirky home, we're wild and free.

Under the roof where the laughter grows,
Every day brings amusing woes.
Together we dance with reckless cheer,
In this funny patch, we hold each dear.

Graceful Anticipation in the Thicket

In the garden, a squirrel thinks,
Stashing acorns, plotting links.
With a dash and cheeky grin,
He races out, his dance begins.

The daisies giggle, they know the score,
While bees argue over who flies more.
With a hop and a whirl, oh such delight,
Nature's party begins at twilight.

The rabbits gather, in joyous cheer,
Cracking jokes about the lack of deer.
They munch on greens, oh what a sight,
As shadows stretch and day turns night.

In this thicket, laughter sways,
Time slips past in the silliest ways.
With antics found in every nook,
Life's a quirky, lovely, playful book.

The Odyssey of Our Roots

Our garden's a ship, so tall and wide,
The carrots stand tall, our trusty guide.
With potatoes deep in a muddy trench,
They whisper tales, oh so drenched.

The tomatoes blush under rough skins,
As colors bang drums where joy begins.
Cucumbers plotting a leafy spree,
While the old oak chuckles, 'Look at me!'

The daisies hold court, a blooming dance,
With petals swirling, they take a chance.
And every worm tells a joke quite crude,
As they wiggle around, in earthy mood.

Together they flourish, united and proud,
Sending roots deep, above which they crowd.
In this banquet of growth, we join the fun,
Who knew gardening could weigh a ton?

Refuge Made of Dreams

In a patch beneath the old tall tree,
The ants hold meetings, won't let me see.
With secret plans and tiny suits,
Plotting the great grape and beet pursuits.

A sleepy cat, with comical snores,
Takes up the space, masters of wars.
The lizards debate, looking quite grand,
On how to lay claim to this sandy land.

The clouds float by in fluffy attire,
While the sun tickles leaves with warm desire.
A gathering of voices, loud and sweet,
In our laughter, all chaos meets.

A refuge made of giggles and glee,
Where dreams take root on every tree.
In this whimsical realm, we'll forever thrive,
With fun as a mission, we come alive!

A Bough of Tranquility

A branch bends low, with a wink and grin,
Inviting us up for some fun within.
Birds chirp low, gossiping fast,
While clouds drift by, shadows they cast.

The wind tells tales of silly finds,
And nature hums with playful minds.
Dancing leaves, a breezy tease,
It's hard to stay calm when the branches squeeze.

The saplings sway in a tiny dance,
Chasing the bees in a lively prance.
With laughter echoing through the air,
How can we not join, shedding our cares?

So up we go, with giggles and might,
A bough of tranquility, what a sight!
In this peaceful haven, where fun won't cease,
We find our joy, our heart's release.

The Canopy of Kindred Hearts

Beneath the leafy vault, we play,
Laughter echoes, bright and gay.
Squirrels eye our picnic spread,
Hoping for a crumb or shred.

Branches sway like happy dancers,
Tickled by the breeze's prancers.
We dodge a raindrop, laugh with glee,
Befriend a beetle, sip our tea.

The giggles of the birds align,
With our jokes and comic signs.
A raccoon rolls its eyes in jest,
As we toast to this merry fest.

Each shadow dances, casting fun,
Cheerful thoughts beneath the sun.
In this shelter, sweet and bright,
We find our joy, our sheer delight.

Luminescence in the Underbrush

Glowworms light up our evening meal,
They're the chefs, their dance surreal.
A firefly winks, our chef encore,
'For dessert, I'll bring you more!'

With ants as waiters, skillful, spry,
They hustle round, oh my oh my!
'One more drink!' we shout on cue,
The ants just shrug, 'We'll bring a few!'

A bushy tail brings in the cake,
With frosting made from berry shake.
It's all quite silly, we all agree,
A woodland feast, so wild and free.

As laughter bounces off the trees,
We toast with cups of dandelion breeze.
In every rustle, joy's our guide,
In this glow, we take our pride.

Harmony in the High Branches

Perched upon these branches high,
We spot a raccoon winking sly.
It steals our snacks, a furry thief,
Yet we can't help but laugh, in disbelief!

A parrot squawks, "You owe me toast!"
While we just chuckle, it's a roast!
With leafy greens our only grace,
Each meal becomes a silly race.

The sun peeks through, a golden ray,
We dance like leaves, come what may.
In jig and jiggle, we twirl around,
With giggles bursting, joy is found.

Nature's quirks, our playful glee,
In every branch, a jubilee.
With laughter soaring, hearts so bright,
We claim this space, our pure delight.

Hues of Home and Heart

Our canvas hangs in colors bold,
With crayons stuck, and stories told.
A mischief-maker sprinkles paint,
A muddy paw, the final saint!

With laughter mixed, a lovely hue,
Our shenanigans, a vibrant brew.
A squirrel critiques, "That's overdone!"
"Let's add some wild!"—the war's begun.

Sunlight drips through the leafy vest,
As our little tribe, eyes aglow, we jest.
A turtle joins, slow but spry,
"Might I suggest a splash on high?"

Yet here we thrive in tangled cheer,
In every color, love draws near.
With joy ablaze, our hearts inform,
That in this chaos, we find warm.

The Evergreen Embrace

In a forest thick with cheer,
The squirrels dance, no sign of fear.
A raccoon steals my lunch, oh dear!
But laughter's all that I hold near.

The trees wink with their leafy disguise,
While chipmunks plot their grand surprise.
My worries vanish, just like flies,
In nature's midst, oh how time flies!

The branches sway, a gentle tease,
As laughter floats upon the breeze.
We chase the shadows, roll with ease,
In this wild place, we're sure to please.

With friends beside, we climb so high,
Playing hide and seek, we touch the sky.
The sun dips low, it's time to fly,
But memories linger, oh my, oh my!

A Place Where Hearts Collide

In a garden where the daisies wave,
Two hearts collide, oh what a save!
A bee buzzes, thinking it's brave,
While love's like sunlight, warm and rave.

We trip on roots, the laughter swells,
Amid the flowers, our hopes tell.
Each twist and turn, a giggle spells,
In this wild tale where friendship dwells.

A froggy friend leaps with a grin,
We dance like bugs, the fun begins.
With every bloom, we shed our skin,
In this odd place, we're always kin.

As twilight falls, we swap our dreams,
In firefly lights, our joy redeems.
A world so funny, bursting at the seams,
Here's to the love in wildest themes!

Pathways Carved in Time

Through winding trails, with laughter loud,
We skip and hop, so very proud.
The trees stand tall like nature's crowd,
Mapping our journeys like a cloud.

We lost a shoe, the mud is fine,
A duck quacks off, "Hey, that's my line!"
With every step, our spirits shine,
These silly paths are surely divine.

The flowers giggle, sway in glee,
While mud pies fly far, just wait and see!
A path of joy is where we'll be,
An adventure wrapped in mystery.

With every twist, the fun unfolds,
In each small moment, laughter molds.
On this wild ride, our story holds,
As time ticks by, our heartbeats bold!

The Symphony of Growth and Glee

In gardens bright where laughter sings,
A symphony of joy takes wing.
The cosmos blooms, with joy it flings,
As even grumpy frogs want bling.

We plant our dreams in soil so rich,
Each sprout a laugh, each bud a pitch.
Mismatched shoes and hair a hitch,
In this grand play, we're quite the niche.

Comedies bloom with every sprout,
With friends around, there's never doubt.
In this wild tuning, all about,
We grow like weeds, and that's no bout.

As sun sinks low, and twilight glows,
Our hearts unite, and laughter flows.
In this wild symphony, love grows,
We dance along, as happiness shows!

Echoes of Laughter and Love

In a warm corner where soft pillows rest,
Laughter bubbles, it's the best quest.
Cats chase shadows, dogs steal the show,
Mom's secret cookies get nibbled, oh no!

Ticklish toes peek from blankets each night,
Sibling whispers fade into light.
Dancing in socks, we trip and we fall,
Echoes of giggles bounce off the wall.

Safe Haven of Breezy Nooks

In a shady nook where the breeze sings low,
Grandpa's old stories take us where we go.
A hammock sways, like a cloud in the air,
Whispers of mischief float everywhere.

Grapevine tales mix with sips of sweet tea,
The dog steals a sandwich, what a sight to see!
Laughter erupts as the cat gives a leap,
In this cozy corner, we're safe as we sleep.

A Sanctuary of Runs and Routes

Through winding paths where the sunbeams play,
Each twist reveals what's planned for the day.
We sprint through the grass, trying hard not to trip,
But pizza runs wild on our tasty grip.

Ducklings parade, waddle here and there,
Kids chase after, with giggles to spare.
Racing the wind, who can hop the best?
Turns out it's the dog, who's always a jest!

The Spice of Nature's Love

In the garden where the tomatoes thrive,
We hold a contest to see who's most alive.
A sprinkle of dirt on each nose, what a sight,
Next snack's a salad, oh what pure delight!

The squirrels plot raids on our sunny feast,
But their acrobatics bring laughter, at least.
Nature's a chef with her pots and her smiles,
It's the spice of our days, bringing joy in piles.

The Tree of Us

In a tree where we dwell,
Laughter drips like rain,
Squirrels throw acorns down,
As if it's all a game.

Branches twist and bend,
Like our silly dance,
Leaves whisper secrets,
Of our clumsy romance.

The bark tells our stories,
Of picnics gone wrong,
When ants stole our snacks,
And we burst into song.

So here we shall stay,
In our leafy embrace,
Amidst nature's laughter,
This unforgettable place.

Canopy of Care

Beneath the leafy roof,
We've got our own spot,
Where pinecones fall like raindrops,
And laughter counts a lot.

Mom's cookies get stuck,
In the branches above,
The raccoons hold a summit,
Saying they're sweet and love!

Dad tries to climb high,
But slips on a twig,
We can't help but giggle,
As he does a little jig.

Yet here in this shade,
We gather and play,
In our silly little world,
Care makes every day.

A Tapestry of Twigs

A patchwork of branches,
Woven tight with joy,
Birds drop notes like letters,
To tease our little boy.

Leaves tell tall tales,
Of our wild backyard,
Where chaos reigns supreme,
And peace is kinda hard.

In the mess of twigs,
We've built a small fort,
But squirrels have claimed it,
For their nutty resort.

Yet laughter is knitted,
In this quirky design,
A tapestry of giggles,
With love by every vine.

The Heartbeat Beneath the Maple

Beneath our big maple,
Where we make a fuss,
The shadows dance to music,
Where summers become us.

The squirrels make a ruckus,
Chasing tails in a whirl,
While we can't stop laughing,
Watching their silly twirl.

Daddy's head gets stuck,
In our hammock so wide,
Mom says he looks funny,
As we swing side to side.

Yet in this warm heartbeat,
We laugh and we jive,
Together in the shade,
This is where we thrive.

Stories Woven in Green

In the park where squirrels prance,
Telling tales of nutty romance.
Trees gossip with the breeze's spin,
While ants march home, their victory grin.

Beneath the leaves, a child's delight,
Chasing shadows, what a sight!
A ladybug dons a tiny crown,
As giggles soar and never drown.

Grass tickles toes and makes them dance,
While hidden frogs fake their stance.
A secret told by a laughing tree,
Says, "Life's too short, come play with me!"

So gather 'round, let stories bloom,
In the heart where all is room.
For each leaf holds a silly tale,
Of triumphant jumps and puppy tails.

Refuge Among the Rustling Foliage

Where branches wave and shadows tease,
A raccoon steals snacks with utmost ease.
"Finders keepers!" he declares with a wink,
While birds in chorus chirp and clink.

Beneath the boughs, a picnic spread,
With watermelon rinds and crumbs of bread.
The ants line up, a dedicated crew,
As one shouts, "Hey! We want some too!"

A child's laughter rings so clear,
As butterflies flutter, oh so near.
"Don't eat the cake!" the mom does shout,
While the dog plots to sneak it out.

So let's embrace this leafy bliss,
Where chaos blooms with every kiss.
For in this green, with joys so bold,
Are secrets known to leaf and old.

Nestled in Nature's Arms

In a hammock hanging just right,
A cat swings softly, what a sight!
She dreams of fish and clouds made of tuna,
As laughter bubbles, a joyful tune-a.

A hedgehog dons a party hat,
Stealing snacks — oh, imagine that!
He rolls away with each delight,
While birds compete in a silly fight.

Giggling children give chase to bees,
Dodging flowers, squealing, "Please!"
Under the sun, there's mischief and fun,
As laughter echoes, no need to run.

So gather round in nature's clasp,
With stories shared, a friendly gasp.
For every hush beneath these trees,
Hides tales of joy and everlasting ease.

Shadows of Comfort

Where sunbeams dance upon the floor,
And shadows leap, eager for more.
A rabbit hops with a mischief grin,
As chubby squirrels plot their win.

A father reads beneath the shade,
While kids make forts — a great escapade!
Leaves rustle softly, a gentle cheer,
As a bee buzzes by, fighting fear.

In blankets wrapped, the laughter spreads,
With snacks aplenty, the fun life leads.
A dog rolls over, snoring loud,
As the sun sets, a sleepy crowd.

So linger long, let tales unfold,
In the arms of nature, warmth so bold.
For every giggle, a memory made,
In the shadows where joys cascade.

A Home of Whispered Wishes

In corners where dust bunnies play,
Laughter dances on shelves each day.
The cat performs a tightrope act,
While socks have gone missing—that's a fact!

Three spoons in the drawer, who took the rest?
The kitchen's now hosting a spoon-wrestling fest.
We gather 'round for a culinary treat,
With burnt toast triumph and recipes sweet!

The chair squeaks like it's got a sore back,
While kids hide snacks in a secretive pack.
The fridge hums a song, old and wise,
With leftovers hiding in clever disguise!

At dusk, we unleash our wild, goofy side,
As the dog plots his escape outside.
In a home full of whimsy and lighthearted play,
Love lingers in laughter at the end of the day.

Three Knots of Connection

A sock here, a shoe there, a jumbled craze,
We weave our lives in comical ways.
With your quirks and my giggles, we tie it tight,
Three knots of connection under the moonlight.

Tea spills on the table, a sketch gone awry,
One sneeze leads to cake flying high.
In our light-hearted chaos, we find our grace,
A tapestry woven in this messy place.

The plants gossip leaves that they're having a ball,
While the lamp with a wobble gives a shine to us all.
We share our odd stories with colorful flair,
Each giggle a thread, in our tales laid bare.

While laundry mounts up like a mountain tall,
We dance through the rooms, answering the call.
Three hearts intertwined in this funny old dome,
Finding magic and laughter, forever our home.

A Breath in Every Bough

In the living room's glow, shadows start to sway,
The plant on the shelf insists it's here to stay.
It's inhaling our secrets, exhaling delight,
A life we embrace, with love taking flight.

The dog snores symphonies, a comical tune,
While I ponder the mysteries of spoons and a moon.
Each room's a riddle wrapped up in glee,
Like socks playing hide-and-seek, oh can't you see?

In the kitchen, pandemonium reigns supreme,
As flour fights back in a powdered dream.
A breath in the air, laughter does bloom,
In this silly circus we call our home room.

With echoes of giggles against the wall's grace,
Every hiccup of joy finds a cozy place.
Among mismatched cushions, a tapestry spun,
In each shared heartbeat, we shine, oh what fun!

Unraveled as One

The clock on the wall ticks in quirky rhymes,
We dance through the days, laughing between times.
The couch speaks of battles with popcorn debris,
As we plot our escape to the land of the free.

With blankets all tangled, we ambush the night,
In pajamas adorned with cartoonish insights.
The dog dreams of tacos, a whimsical chase,
As we share silly grins and a warm embrace.

The roof creaks a serenade familiar and sweet,
While dinner's a gala of mismatched meat.
Each slice of the pie comes with a side of jest,
Creating a portrait of laughter's great quest.

With crayons and doodles we lay our plans,
For adventures on trips to faraway lands.
So here's to the funny and silly we've spun,
In this tangle of chaos, we're unraveled as one.

Embrace of Whispering Leaves

In the backyard, squirrels scheme,
While birds gossip, it feels like a dream.
Rabbits hop with their fluffy tails,
Chasing shadows and elusive trails.

A raccoon winks, swiping snacks,
Stealing my sandwich, clever and relaxed.
The garden gnome rolls his eyes,
As the sun tickles with playful skies.

Laughter echoes through trees so tall,
Where branches sway and secrets call.
Nature's jesters put on a show,
In this lively circus, joy will grow.

Under the arch of leafy green,
Funny moments are often seen.
Home's silly tales and laughter shared,
Caught in the breeze, all unprepared.

Sheltering Shadows of Memory

In the shade where the stories twist,
A sunburnt dog naps, too tired to resist.
Grandma's hat flutters, a silly clown,
While grandkids giggle, running around.

Chasing shadows, they trip and fall,
Landing in laughter, a light-hearted brawl.
A kite gets caught in the old oak tree,
A moment of triumph, then it's all spree.

The swing creaks like it's got a joke,
As old leaves whisper and branches poke.
Memory drips like lemonade sweet,
A taste of sunlight, pure and neat.

In this refuge where laughter gleams,
Funny moments are woven in dreams.
Stories live in the gentle sway,
Of shadowed reminders of a playful day.

Beneath the Natural Arch

Where trees bow low and the sun peeks,
Funny echoes play hide and seek.
A squirrel's acrobatics steal the show,
While ants hold their tiny disco below.

Pine cones drop like clumsy bombs,
As grasshoppers dance to the earth's sweet psalms.
The breeze chuckles, inviting all,
Join the revelry—no need to stall!

Leaves rustle with a wink and cheer,
Nature's antics merry and clear.
Kids dress up as explorers bold,
With sticks for swords and tales retold.

Beneath the arch where laughter springs,
Every heartbeat curiously sings.
Life's a carnival, bright and grand,
In this world, hand in hand.

Hearth of Hidden Dreams

Around the fire, we roast some laughs,
With marshmallows piling like fun-sized staffs.
The stories swirl with a smoky flair,
As shadows giggle and jump in the air.

Dad tells tales that defy the years,
Of sneaky pets and childhood fears.
While laughter bounces off the walls,
Echoing magic as the evening calls.

Fireflies buzz with shiny delight,
Joining the jesters in the sparkling night.
A brave raccoon with a boon of snacks,
Turns us from friends to playful hacks!

In this heart of whimsy, dreams ignite,
While hidden giggles keep us light.
Laughter and love in the gentle glow,
Remind us where our true roots grow.

The Beauty of Sheltered Serenity

In a world where squirrels plot,
They hoard all nuts, like it's their lot.
Birds gossip secrets high above,
While the dog just dreams of love.

The branches sway with laughter bright,
As the sun dips low, a golden light.
Mice host parties, oh what a scene!
Dancing on leaves, it's quite the routine!

A cat winks, plotting his sneak,
As kids run wild, giggles they tweak.
The old tree groans, sharing its tales,
While ants march by on unknown trails.

So here we stand, beneath this jest,
Nature's humor is at its best.
With every rustle, a chuckle's born,
In our shared realm, we laugh 'til dawn.

Harmony in the Fragrant Underbrush

Frogs croak songs of silly hopes,
In muddy boots, we dance like dopes.
The flowers bloom, with colors grand,
As bees perform their buzzing band.

Mushrooms peek from the leafy floor,
With faces like they've seen much more.
A hedgehog rolls, in quite a spin,
While the lilacs giggle, wearing a grin.

The wind whispers with playful flair,
Tickling leaves, a gentle care.
Oh, to be a part of the play,
Where laughter breaths the light of day!

With every step, mischief sneaks,
Nature's quirks bring out our peaks.
We roam this patch, a joyful crush,
Where every bush has secrets to hush.

A Retreat in the Cradle of Trees

Beneath the boughs of leafy dreams,
A squirrel steals my candy creams.
He scuttles up with quite the speed,
As I just watch, oh yes indeed!

The grasses giggle with every breeze,
Dandelions dance, they'll do as they please.
A rabbit pops up, with a wink and a hop,
While the wise old owl gives a thoughtful drop.

Sunlight dapples on forest floors,
As little critters open their doors.
Ants throw parties under the thorns,
While I indulge in sweet by-corns!

With laughter shared, we dwell as one,
A patchwork quilt of nature's fun.
So let's embrace this playful rhyme,
In this cozy nook, there's always time.

When Nature's Lullaby Calls

Twilight brings a sleepy song,
As crickets chirp, they hum along.
The fireflies paint the dusky scene,
While frogs croon softly, evergreen.

In cozy nooks, the faeries play,
With whispered giggles, they fly away.
A raccoon dines on leftover pie,
While I just watch, oh my, oh my!

The wind plays tricks, with my hat it steals,
And twirling leaves dance in squeals.
So gather 'round, let laughter roll,
In this space where our hearts feel whole.

As the stars peek out, we'll share a laugh,
Nature's blanket—our cozy half.
When the lullaby beckons us near,
We find the humor that brings us cheer.

Roots That Hold Us Firm

In a garden where laughter grows,
We dig deep, where the wild grass knows.
Silly flowers dance in the rain,
Chasing the sun, oh what a gain!

With socks on the line, a sight to see,
A squirrel cheers us on, just like he.
Roots intertwine, a heartwarming game,
Silly tales of the day, never the same.

The garden gnomes roll their eyes with glee,
As we tell tales of the one banana tree.
Under their noses, the laughter flows,
In this patch of love, our joy simply glows.

Beneath the moonlit winks and sighs,
We grow side by side, oh, how time flies!
A family tree with quirks to show,
Together we giggle, together we grow.

Swaying in the Breeze of Belonging

Up in the treehouse, we plan our spree,
Swinging on branches, wild and free.
With a banana peel slip and a loud shout,
Even the squirrels are laughing, no doubt!

It's always a party when we all show,
Races with ants, oh, where did they go?
With branches that sway, we giggle in glee,
As the wind joins in, it's a wild jubilee.

Mismatched socks on our feet in dismay,
We twirl around, hip-hop and sway.
Dancing like leaves in a breezy play,
Home is the stage where we laugh and stay.

So come take a seat on our rickety throne,
With laughter as royal, we're never alone.
In this messy nest where we lounge and sing,
Together we sway, with joy as our king!

The Gathering of Wild Spirits

In the clamor of pots with a bellyful cheer,
We gather like birds, oh, what brings us near?
With a pie made of giggles and laughter so sweet,
Even the cat thinks it's time for a treat!

Along comes the dog, with a wagging tail,
Stealing our sandwiches without fail.
The parrot squawks, joining our song,
In this ball of chaos, we all belong.

Who needs a plan when we've got the fun?
Let's roll in the mud, oh, who's got the sun?
With a splash and a laugh, the wild spirit sings,
Together we soar on the backs of our wings.

Every mishap makes the story complete,
In this crazy crew, life's never discreet.
From sparkles and spills to the charms of the day,
We gather as one; what a grand, funny play!

The Sweetness of Silent Company

In the quiet nook with a book and a sip,
A treasure of stillness, as shadows do flip.
Cuddled on couches, we share little dreams,
In moments so sweet, life's rhythm redeems.

The cat curls up, stealing the light,
As we whisper soft tales into the night.
A laugh bounces back, oh, what a delight,
In silence we giggle, hearts open and bright.

With tasty snacks piled high on the chair,
Munching together, we float in the air.
Even the clock tickles time with a grin,
In cozy spaces, where whimsy begins.

Though words may be few, we feel the embrace,
In shared quiet moments, we find our place.
With gentle smiles and the warmth of a hug,
In this tender refuge, we're all snug as a bug!

Isle of Safe Shores

On this isle of sandy dreams,
Where seagulls steal our ice cream.
We dodge waves like they're old friends,
And laugh until the daylight ends.

The crabs dance in tiny shoes,
While sunburned folks sip on brews.
Shells whisper secrets of the sea,
Let's host a party, just you and me.

Palm trees sway with comic flair,
They throw shade like they just don't care.
Each sunset's a sitcom rerun,
Filled with laughter, never a pun.

So grab a kite, let's touch the sky,
We'll fly our troubles way up high.
This isle's a haven, come take your seat,
With giggles and sunshine, life is sweet.

Leafy Embrace

Beneath branches, squirrels conspire,
While ants form a line, a crazed choir.
The leaves rustle, gossip goes 'round,
"Who borrowed my acorn? It's not found!"

A snail slides by with stylish flair,
Thinking it's the next big fair.
While frogs debate on whose croak's loud,
In this leafy embrace we're all proud.

One tree swings its branches wide,
And all the critters dash inside.
From woodpeckers drumming, to dogs that play,
It's a nature-made cabaret every day!

We sip our tea, and watch the show,
With laughter that bubbles, and joy that flows.
Surrounded by greens and nature's cheer,
In this leafy embrace, there's nothing to fear.

Nest of the Earth's Sisters

In a nest high up in the trees,
Sisters chirp with mischievous tease.
They share tales of acorns and dreams,
While plotting great heists with silly schemes.

One squirrel claims to sight a throne,
Made of twigs and glittering stones.
But as they plan, one slips, oh dear!
Lands right in a pie — what a cheer!

The owls just hoot and roll their eyes,
At the antics and the wild highs.
While ladybugs giggle, they think it's grand,
This nest of sisters, a raucous band.

As dusk falls gently, they all dive in,
For a goodnight story, let the giggles begin.
With starlight above and joy at our side,
In this nest, there's nothing to hide.

The Shade of Our Collective Heart

In the shade where laughter's grown,
Under the porch, we find our throne.
With lemonade and stories shared,
Fun erupts like a joke declared.

The cat struts with an air of pride,
As if to say, "Now, come inside!"
While kids play chase, with giggles loud,
In this shade, we're all so proud.

Grandma's tales, with twists and turns,
Teach us well, as wisdom burns.
While laughter echoes among each bark,
This shade's our shelter, our joyous park.

As fireflies start to light the night,
We dance and twirl, oh, what a sight!
In shade's embrace, our hearts align,
In laughter and love, everything's fine.

Sunlight Filtering Through Memories

In the attic, a box of hats,
Which I wore while pretending to be cats.
A mishmash of memories stir and spin,
Laughter echoes loud, where did I begin?

Sunshine spills through the crooked door,
Tickling the dust on the wooden floor.
Whispers of toys that I thought I lost,
Now dance with shadows, not caring the cost.

Socks from my childhood, mismatched yet bright,
Roll in the sun like a warm summer kite.
Every corner holds a story so grand,
In the glint of the glass, adventures are planned.

Oh, the smell of the cookies, burnt but sweet,
A recipe called chaos, now quite a treat.
Each bite's a journey, a history fed,
In the garden of laughter, we'll never tread.

Home Among the Moss

Squishy green carpets under my feet,
Moss tickles toes in a natural greet.
Chatty squirrels gossip from bough to bough,
While I try to blend in - look at me now!

The tree to my left gives a knowing wink,
I swear I can hear it, what do you think?
A dance of the ferns in a soft, silly breeze,
While I trip on my shoelace and stumble with ease.

The raccoons join in for a late-night feast,
Swiping the snacks like they're hosting a beast.
But they tiptoe and tumble, oh what a sight,
As the stars wink down, casting giggles in night.

I set up my camp with a blanket and cheer,
Chasing the giggles that float through the sphere.
A kingdom of quirks where the laughter runs free,
Home among moss, just my friends and me.

Breaths of Wild Serenity

The breeze tickles noses with scents of the earth,
While birds throw a party, oh what a mirth!
I trip over roots while I mimic a deer,
Nature laughs gently as I disappear.

Dandelions giggle, they bloom with a grin,
As I blow all their wishes, where to begin?
A badge of odd honor, the pollen I wear,
My sneezes become tunes in the wild, oh beware!

Clouds join the ruckus, becoming a stage,
As I tell them my secrets, they laugh in a rage.
Sunbeams take selfies, capturing me,
A wild serenade, oh what glee!

In this verdant realm, I'm king of the jest,
With butterflies dancing, I laugh with the best.
Each breath a new giggle, each moment a cheer,
In this wild sanctuary, there's nothing to fear.

Embraced by Nature's Guardian

A tree with a beard, so wise and so grand,
Winks at my folly, lends me a hand.
Bark tickles my back while I laugh with delight,
Nature's guardian chuckles, oh what a sight!

The sun plays peek-a-boo, dodging the leaves,
While critters conspire in creative reprieves.
I see a hare dancing, a floppy knee bend,
Nature's all-party, where chaos won't end.

Butterflies flutter, they take to the air,
While I'm twisted up in my long curly hair.
"Help!" I declare, but they giggle in flight,
In this realm of wildness, all wrongs turn to right.

Oh, what jests play beneath branches so wide,
With laughter and silliness always onside.
Embraced by a conscience that's whimsy and cheer,
I'm at home with the quirks, in the wild, oh so dear.

Treehouse Dreams and Soaring Hopes

In a treehouse high, we build our fort,
Where squirrels debate the latest sport.
The owl gives a hoot, what a wise guy,
While we make plans to soar and fly.

With snacks piled high, we hold our feast,
A peanut butter sandwich is quite the beast.
We giggle at shadows, dance like the breeze,
And all our laughter brings us to our knees.

The leaves sway gently, a whispering song,
Nature chuckles, for nothing feels wrong.
As we swing from branches, dreams take flight,
Under the stars, we have all night.

So raise your juice box, toast to the trees,
May our secret hideouts be filled with glee.
For in this kingdom of branches and beams,
We're rulers of laughter and childhood dreams.

Harmony of Nature's Blanket

A blanket of leaves wraps us so tight,
While ants march past, a curious sight.
The sun spills fun with a playful grin,
As we find treasures where the wild things spin.

We're the keepers of secrets, silly and grand,
While a butterfly sneezes, oh, isn't that planned?
Nature's a circus with frogs in a show,
Each hop's a performance, a standard to bow.

In this little world, we dance on the grass,
Where clouds are pillows, and time seems to pass.
A snail takes a selfie, it's all the rage,
As we flip through our laughter on this silly stage.

With birds in a choir singing off-key,
We giggle and snicker, just you and me.
So snuggle up close in this silly spot,
Where harmony blooms and worries are not.

Tapestry of Roots and Wings

Beneath the trees, we sketch our plans,
With crayons from nature and twigs for bands.
We invent a world where giggles grow,
And squirrels recite all the gossip they know.

A tapestry woven, with stories to share,
Of a raccoon dressed fine in a top hat and chair.
We map out the clouds, paint skies full of cheer,
In our wacky adventures, we show no fear.

The roots tickle toes, like a game of tag,
While a frog in a cape takes his victory brag.
With laughter as glue, we bind it all tight,
Our imaginations soar, oh, what a delight!

So let's fly with dreams, on the back of a breeze,
With roots holding firm, and hearts at ease.
For in this wild place, we're stars in the show,
With a whimsical spirit, off we will go.

Where the Wildflowers Greet

In a field filled with wildflowers, a feast of color,
We dance like bees, humming our own vigor.
Dandelions whisper secrets of cheer,
While sunbeams play tag and butterflies leer.

A ladybug giggles, dressed up in spots,
With petals as pillows, we plot silly plots.
The grass tickles toes, oh, what a delight,
As we spin in circles beneath midday light.

Our hats made of leaves, we wear with pride,
As we launch our paper boats down the slide.
With mischief aplenty, the world is a stage,
Where laughter erupts like a wild rampage.

So join in this waltz with roots at our feet,
Amid blossoms and sunbeams, our worries retreat.
For in this wild dance, life's just a treat,
Where smiles grow wild and wildflowers greet.

The Melodies of Green

The tree frogs croak in chatty glee,
Squirrels dance like they're on TV,
Leaves rustle softly, gossiping fun,
While ants march in line, under the sun.

A parrot squawks a riddle today,
A goat on a branch, who's there to stay?
Acorns drop with a comical plop,
Nature's slapstick, it never will stop.

A chipmunk in shades takes a sip,
At the acorn café, he takes a dip,
While bunnies attempt the moonlit prance,
With moves that'll surely make you glance.

With every leaf that's tickled and torn,
There's laughter in a world reborn,
A harmony wrapped in greens and hues,
The essence of joy, in every muse.

Hummingbird Memories

A hummingbird zips by, zooming fast,
Wearing tiny sneakers, what a blast!
It hovers like it's stuck in the air,
Drinking nectar, it doesn't seem to care.

Bumblesbees laugh at their sips so sweet,
While butterflies jiggle on wobbly feet,
A dandelion sneezes, sends seeds a-flight,
And giggles escape as they take off in spite.

Mice gather round for a cozy tale,
Of how they dodged that last sneaky snail,
A caper unfolds under vivid blooms,
As laughter erupts from dark leafy rooms.

Every flutter brings a chuckle or cheer,
Nature's band plays with love sincere,
In unison, they form a bright array,
Memories made in every light-hearted play.

A Shield of Fern and Fable

Beneath the ferns, a storytelling nook,
Where crickets chirp, and the raccoons look,
A hedgehog narrates a love that once was,
While everyone listens, just because.

Snails in tuxedos make quite the show,
In a garden of gossip, oh what a flow!
Their slimy trails tell tales of the night,
While fireflies flicker, putting up a light.

Turtles in glasses ponder life's quest,
With a slow-motion debate, it's quite the jest,
Beetles dress up for a disco affair,
Twisting and twirling without a care.

Every fern holds a laugh, each shadow a grin,
In the fabric of stories, we all fit in,
Together we weave our whimsical threads,
Under the cloak where laughter spreads.

The Cloak of Togetherness

Beneath the branches, we gather and play,
The games of the forest, hip-hip-hooray!
A porcupine juggles, quite the bold act,
While others just cheer, "That's quite a pact!"

The raccoons will deal out cards with flair,
While owls watch closely from high in their lair,
A wild party starts as the sun dips low,
With tickles of laughter, it's quite the show.

Squirrels share tales of the ones they chased,
Each epic encounter, hilariously paced,
Together we dance, our hearts intertwined,
In a cloak of camaraderie, blissfully blind.

As stars sprinkle laughter across the sky,
We toast with dew drops, oh my, oh my!
In this playful haven, we find our right home,
With silliness swirling, wherever we roam.

Roots of Comfort in the Breeze

In a chair with squeaks and rust,
I sip my drink, it's a must.
Squirrels dance upon the grass,
Chasing tails as moments pass.

My dog inspires a chase so bold,
Chasing shadows, stories told.
A blanket fort made of delight,
We stay up late, we laugh all night.

Neighbors peek with curious eyes,
What's that ruckus? Oh, surprise!
Laughter echoes, we're a team,
In this place, we live the dream.

Roots are deep, we stand our ground,
In silliness, true joy is found.
So let's gather, share our bread,
Under trees, life's lightly spread.

Wanderlust Beneath the Wooden Above

A picnic spread where ants parade,
Delicious crumbs are often laid.
The sun peeks in, the shadows play,
In this wonderland, we'll stay.

A kite takes flight; it's lost, oh no!
Up in the branches, it won't show.
Laughter bursts like fireworks bright,
Silly adventures take their flight.

Slip on grass, fall with a thud,
We start anew, bounce like a bud.
With giggles shared 'neath wooden beams,
Our lives entwined in joyful dreams.

So let's explore each nook and cranny,
Sometimes silly, always uncanny.
Under branches, still we roam,
In this place, we've made our home.

When Breezes Carry Love

A feather floats upon the breeze,
Plays tag with leaves, oh what a tease!
With laughter ringing loud and clear,
We spill our secrets, share our cheer.

Who needs a map, we've got our feet?
Each tumble brings a brand new feat.
We'll dance on grass till nightfall calls,
In this joy, our laughter sprawls.

Let's twirl beneath the painted sky,
With friends like these, we'll fly so high.
A breeze of humor fills the space,
Warmth encircled in each embrace.

When breezes carry what we seek,
A comedy of fun, unique.
Together bound by giggles so light,
We're anchored here; it feels just right.

Sanctuary of Dappled Sunlight

The shade is cool, the hearth is warm,
A perfect place to start a charm.
With coffee sips and grandpa's tales,
In this haven, laughter sails.

The cat rolls over, claims a spot,
In the sunlight, it hits the spot.
Silly antics, playful ways,
Make every hour feel like play.

Bouncing ideas like a ball,
We invent worlds, we have a ball.
No need for scripts or staged design,
In the free flow, our hearts align.

So here we gather, day by day,
In dappled sunlight, we will stay.
Our sanctuary of joy and quirk,
Life's simple pleasures—oh, who needs work?

Echoes of the Hearth

In the kitchen, pots will dance,
While the dog attempts a prance.
Cookies burn, but who's to care?
With laughter echoing everywhere!

Grandma's tales, a twist and turn,
We hang on every word, we yearn.
Pasta flops and sauces fly,
And we just shrug, oh my, oh my!

Secrets in the Shade

The backyard hides a jungle gym,
Where squirrels plot and children swim.
A slide that squeaks like an old man's chair,
And sticky fingers tucked in hair.

In the shade, the gossip grows,
Who ate the pie? Nobody knows!
Lemonade spills on dad's old cap,
And laughter's the best, cozy trap.

The Embrace of Familiar Roots

Roots stretch deep beneath the ground,
But it's the daisies we've found!
Worms in racecars speed on by,
While ants plan parties, oh my, oh my!

Grandpa's plant is now a tree,
With eyes that watch, both wise and free.
A hammock sways where dreams collide,
With snacks nearby for the wild ride!

Beneath Our Branching Dreams

The branches offer a pillow fight,
As cats and kids take flight each night.
We climb the dreams up to the stars,
While singing loud, to speed our cars.

Laughter spills like milk on grass,
With memories that we will amass.
Under the moon, we twirl and spin,
In our hearts, that's where we begin!

Harmony in the Glistening Canopy

In branches high, we do reside,
With squirrel chatter, and laughs beside.
A dance of leaves, a buzzing bee,
A kite gone rogue, oh what a spree!

A picnic planned, snacks galore,
But ants arrive, we counter more.
With sandwiches and soda spills,
We laugh at our unplanned thrills!

Our dog, a thief of every sock,
He prances round, like he can talk.
We chase him down, oh what a chase,
A comedy in our little space!

Laughter echoes under light,
As shadows stretch into the night.
With fireflies that wink and tease,
We've found our joy, our hearts at ease.

Echoing Family Footsteps

In cozy halls, where echoes call,
We stumble often, trip and fall.
A race ensues, who's fastest here?
My brother's pride turns to a sneer!

Mom's cooking sounds, a mighty roar,
But dad's voice starts a playful war.
Each call to eat, a sneaky trap,
We fight to see who's first for snack!

The dog joins in, a joyful yelp,
He's part of this, in every skelp.
With tails and chairs, we juggle chairs,
A game of chaos, love and cares!

As night falls down, we all reunite,
In dreams of laughter, hearts feel light.
A family bond that always sticks,
In every joke, in every trick.

Flickers of Joy in Shadows

The evening sun casts quirky shapes,
As shadows dance in funny capes.
We create tales of heroes bright,
A cat's adventures in the night!

With flashlights bright, we find our glow,
But dad's behind the curtain, oh no!
A ghostly prank, a playful fright,
We squeal and giggle, such delight!

The trampoline boasts a summer fling,
With cousins leaping, all a-swing.
Who flies the highest? Who takes the prize?
Just watch those socks, they're quite the surprise!

Amid the giggles, sun ends its reign,
As stars peek through, we stop the game.
In whispers shared, with love we bond,
These joyful flickers stretch beyond.

A Hearth for Wandering Souls

With mismatched socks, we gather near,
Each tale of woe turns into cheer.
The sofa's soft, our laughter blends,
A hearth that warms, where love transcends.

Our pet, the king, brings much delight,
He rules the roost, both day and night.
With every bark and snarky glance,
He steals the show, it's clear at a glance!

Mom brews cocoa, but not for all,
She guards her stash—a secret haul!
We bargain hard, the game is set,
The price is high, but it's worth the fret!

Through jests and quirks, we find our way,
A hearth of love that's here to stay.
In laughter bright, we take our place,
Forever bound, in this warm space.

Canopy of Silken Echoes

Beneath the sheets, I hide my face,
Pillow fights, a feathery race.
Laughter blares, a joyful din,
As crumbs of snacks fall on my chin.

Socks mismatched, a fashion faux pas,
Dancing with cats, a grand ol' spa.
The trees above seem to giggle low,
As I trip on roots, putting on a show.

Naps are taken in sunshine's glow,
With ants as guests, putting on a show.
A chorus of chirps, a wild ballet,
Who knew home's chaos could feel so gay?

Where laughter lingers, that's my chair,
With a blanket burrito, life's a rare flair.
Kites on the ceiling, dreams fly fleet,
In the sweet kookiness, my heart skips a beat.

The Nest of Warmth and Light

Cereal spills, a breakfast art,
A masterpiece that plays the part.
With tigers prowling in my room,
I build a fort from couch and broom.

Banana peels become a slide,
With pillows stacked, I take a ride.
The sun seeps in and warm hugs flow,
As I plot mischief with my shadow.

Grandma's cookies in one hand,
A secret stash, oh so grand!
Giggles bounce off walls like balls,
In this sanctuary, giggling calls.

The plants all nod to my silly dance,
With overgrown hair, I dare to prance!
Home's silly rhythms fill the air,
In joyful madness, I find my lair.

Living Under Leafy Embrace

Tangled limbs on my brother's head,
Like leafy vines where dreams are spread.
Hide and seek in shadows play,
Home is where we jest and sway.

Twisted tales from a cracked old book,
The pet goldfish gives a knowing look.
With lazy afternoons, we share a laugh,
Imagining life as a quirky giraffe.

Pizza boxes build a tower high,
While squirrels debate who gets the pie.
Sidewalk chalk paints grand designs,
As our laughter intertwines like vines.

Branches shake with secrets learned,
Stories told, and giggles earned.
In this colorful mess, we belong,
Dancing together, we sing our song.

The Secret Oasis of Belonging

In a den of pillows, we wrap our joy,
Snuggled tight with a favorite toy.
Laughter bubbles like a fizzy drink,
Where silly thoughts are allowed to think.

Toys in a spin, a racing spree,
Chasing ducks that float on tea.
Mom's cooking wafts like a magic spell,
As the dog prances, barking, "Oh, well!"

Under the table, a secret place,
With whispers shared, a cozy space.
Cookies forgotten become a feast,
For a troop of friends, the laughter's increased.

Every corner hides a whimsical tale,
With echoes of giggles that never fail.
This little kingdom where chaos reigns,
Paints a smile on life's transparent panes.

www.ingramcontent.com/pod-product-compliance
Lightning Source LLC
Chambersburg PA
CBHW070320120526
44590CB00017B/2758